Watercolor
A step-by-step guide for art enthusiasts

More than creative packaging

This 2007 edition published by Barnes & Noble, Inc.,
by arrangement with SpiceBox Ltd.

Illustration and text by Philip Berrill,
Photography by Peter Raymond
Design by JW Veldhoen

Barnes & Noble, Inc.
122 Fifth Avenue
New York, NY 10011

ISBN: 978-1-4351-0391-7

Printed and bound in China

5   7   9   10   8   6   4

Contents

About the Author:
Philip Berrill

Philip Berrill is a professional artist, tutor, lecturer, and author—his method for learning to paint taught and enjoyed worldwide. Born in 1945 in Northampton, England, Philip now lives in Southport with his wife Sylvia, and his daughter Penelope.

Philip recalls how he discovered paint at age three. It was a sunny afternoon, he wandered into his father's greenhouse and saw at the far end of the building a large bucket of whitewash, and a tubular pump sprayer. Philip loaded the sprayer, and had a lovely afternoon covering all of his father's best tomatoes and plants with white. He had discovered paint, and that it could change how you see the world.

Author, artist, lecturer, Philip Berrill

At the age of fourteen, Philip decided he would make a living as a professional artist. He came under the influence of the Welsh artist and tutor John Sullivan. Philip held his first solo exhibition at the age of eighteen, followed by other group, and solo exhibitions. At the age of twenty-eight, Liverpool University held a major exhibition of his work — the direct result of which was that Philip could realize his ambition to become a professional artist. He launched very successful art classes using his unique approach to teaching, sketching, and painting. These classes proved so popular Philip went on to develop worldwide correspondence courses. In the 1980s, he embarked on the next stage of his career that led to his being nicknamed The Flying Artist. After offering sought-after painting vacation courses in Great Britain, he organized additional painting holiday retreats in Europe — in Rome, Venice, Florence, and Paris. Subsequently Philip lectured and demonstrated painting in America and the Middle East. Philip's much-admired exhibition, *The Italian Connection*, consists of sketches and paintings from his Italian journeys, and other European locations. Philip's love and enthusiasm for sketching and painting is infectious. He believes that art should be for everyone, and that you are never too young, or too old, to begin sketching. His students have ranged from ten to eighty, and he continues to enjoy passing on his enthusiasm and knowledge, gained over thirty years, to people from all walks of life. Philip has designed his method for people of all ages and all abilities, and over recent years has produced a series of art videos. These videos led to an invitation to produce and present a thirteen-part television series *Paint with the Flying Artist* and that project in turn led to the writing and illustration of this series of art books designed especially for you — books covering a wide range of mediums, techniques, and subjects to introduce you to the joy and pleasure of sketching and painting. These beautifully presented books come with all the materials you will need to get started painting and drawing. The compact form and portability of the kit allows freedom and spontaneity to capture each moment of inspiration that Philip demonstrates in his own work. The hope is that these kits will assist you in your own journey of sketching and painting.

Watercolor of the Piazza San Marco and the Palazzo Ducale

Introduction

How often have you wished that you could paint? From the earliest times, man has drawn and painted. From cave paintings by primitive man in France and Spain to the stylized and beautiful decorative art of the Egyptians; from Byzantine mosaics to great works of the Italian Renaissance such as the Mona Lisa and the Last Supper by Leonardo da Vinci, painting transcends generations, nationalities and ages. Indeed, art transcends language, race or political boundaries and is as much of a pleasure to create as it is to view. Pictures and artwork surround us; they are on the greeting cards that we send and on the book covers we read, on food packages, and fabric designs, pictures are everywhere! They can be funny, serious, moving, calming, challenging or reassuring; pictures, drawings and paintings are part of our everyday life. No wonder so many people say "I wish I could paint." My message to you is: if you want to, you can!

There is no need to be apprehensive about painting. Picasso said at age fifteen he drew and painted like the Italian Master Raphael, but that it took him many more years to learn to paint like a child. If you watch young children, the moment they can pick up a pencil, marker or crayon, they are determined to make marks, to draw and scribble. Quite quickly, by the age of three to four, they start to draw and color the things they see around them, giving their pictures a wonderful degree of expression.

Philip Berrill at work in plein air.

Painting allows a nearly unlimited range of styles and forms. Watercolors especially provide a marvelous means of producing detailed, precise or delicate pictures — or in contrast, bold, quickly painted studies. For example, landscapes capturing the atmospheric effects of rain, mist and sunlight are difficult to obtain in any other medium. Apart from landscapes, watercolors lend themselves to the painting of all subjects including seascapes, still life, portraits, animals and flowers, yet allow for artist's developing of their own style.

Watercolors are an ideal medium to paint for other reasons as well; they require a minimum amount of equipment and involve little, if any, mess. Another nice aspect of watercolor painting is that you don't need a separate room or studio; the materials take up only a small amount of space and can be used on a kitchen or dining room table. They are equally convenient outside or for using indoors.

If you are a beginning painter looking for that boost of confidence and good advice, you will find this book and kit of included supplies are the perfect way to get started exploring this exciting art. Or, if you already sketch or paint, I hope this kit will help to renew your interest, advance your skills, or introduce you to a medium that you may not have tried before, and inspire you with new ideas. I also hope that the compact format of this kit will encourage you to take your painting outdoors and enjoy your pastime in a variety of environments.

People often ask me if painting is a gift only a few possess. My answer to that is no, I firmly believe that the art of being able to sketch and paint is born in everyone. Some people say to me "I would love to paint but I can't draw a straight line." It comes down to motivation. The moment anyone says "I would love to paint," I can assure them that following the right advice and with a little regular practice, they will be able to. I have proven this over and over again with many people of all ages and from all backgrounds. They have taken my advice, followed the demonstrations and techniques, and have become proficient artists in their own right, often producing high-quality work, amazing themselves, their family, and friends. Many have had the great pleasure of seeing their work accepted for exhibition, and have sold paintings. Some have even had their own solo exhibitions. Whether painting solely for your own pleasure and enjoyment, or striving to exhibit, everyone can enjoy the art of painting.

Tom Jones was paralysed in an accident. Philip taught Tom to paint using his mouth.

Materials For Watercolor Painting

During the past thirty to forty years there have been many exciting changes and developments in artists' materials and equipment, more so than the previous three centuries. This has been largely due to advances in the science of color chemistry which have had a significant effect on the materials an artist uses and have opened up new avenues undreamt of by artists of previous generations. The artist now has water soluble pencils, nylon brushes, acrylic and synthetic paints, in addition to the traditional water colors, oil paints and pastels at their disposal. A number of the modern developments benefit today's water color painter.

Water color painting does not need to be expensive. One can start a sketch on the back of an envelope. Art material manufacturers are conscious of both quality and the artist's pocket. They provide top quality materials known as Artists quality, where price is given secondary importance to quality, but ever conscious of the limited finances of many painters and students, they also produce excellent modestly priced paints, brushes and materials.

The Winsor and Newton Artists quality water colors and their Cotman water colors and brushes are fine examples of both qualities. I will describe several ranges of materials within this book for your guidance. A simple rule should be, buy the best art materials you can afford. Painting is a very personal experience and you will find that you come to have favourite brushes, paper and equipment.

Materials For Watercolor Painting

Brushes

It is important to have good quality brushes. The tip of your paint brush is the most important thing between you and your painting. Your paint brushes should be treated with respect and be well cared for, and in return they will give you good service. Your brush should feel like an extension of your fingers. There are ranges of natural hair brushes. Traditionally sable brushes, especially Kolinsky sable, found in the Winsor and Newton series seven range, have been considered by many artists as the best, but the scarcity of high quality sable hair has led to the development of nylon and synthetic brushes. The brushes come in two main shapes, round and flat. The round brushes are usually graded from 0000 to 24 depending on the range. The larger and medium brushes are for general painting and the smaller round brushes are for detail. The flat wash brushes are used for applying large, broad washes of color to your painting. They are normally graded by width from 1/8th" (3mm) to 11/2" (38mm) or wider.

Paint

Water colors are a finely ground mixture of pigment, gum arabic (a water soluble gum from the acacia tree), glycerine (which helps keep the colors moist) and wetting agents (which help the paint flow freely). The paint, when diluted with water on the palette and applied as a wash by brush onto the surface of the paper, has a translucent quality which is a feature of the medium. Paints such as oils or acrylics are essentially opaque and white paint is mixed with the other colors to lighten them. The pure water colorist uses no white paint: water is used to lighten the color and the whiteness of the paper reflects the light through the wash. Water colors are available in three forms; tubes, pans or half pans. Pans and half pans are small, square or rectangular dishes of solid color. Tubes are more convenient for studio use. Color can be squeezed on to the palette from the tube and the color released with a wet brush. Dried out, the paint can be moistened easily with water. Pans of color are convenient for outdoor work because they usually come in sets and are easily portable. Pans are slightly less soluble than tube colors and a little gentle rubbing with the brush is needed to release the colors.

Watercolor Paper

The paper the water color painter uses is very important. I recommend that you use one of the papers specially made for water color painting. Cartridge paper, while ideal for drawing, is too thin for water color painting and can waver and distort when water is applied to it. Water color paper is either made from a wood pulp, from sustainable forests, or from a cotton rag pulp. Both have characteristics all their own. Wood pulp paper is a little less expensive than cotton rag paper. Experiment with both to find the paper which suits you best.

Water color paper surfaces

Water color paper varies in thickness and surface texture. Both offer the artist different options for painting on. The surfaces are HP (Hot Pressed): this is a very smooth surface ideal for detailed work; ROUGH: this has a very pronouced surface and is ideal for bold, free flowing subjects; NOT paper, sometimes referred to as CP (Cold Pressed): this is not rough and not smooth but midway between, and a very popular surface for many water color painters. It is the one I suggest you try first. While water color paper is traditionally white, it is possible to obtain tinted paper. The colored paper has many uses and I will refer to these in a later chapter.

Water color paper thickness

The weight of water color paper is calculated by how much 500 full size Imperial sheets (a ream) of paper weighs. The thicker the sheet, the heavier the paper. Popular water color weights are 90lb. (190gsm), 140lb. (300gsm) and 300lb. (640gsm). I recommend that you work on 140lb. (300gsm) paper with a 'NOT" surface. This is readily obtainable from art stores and art shops in sheet and water color sketch book form. Sheets of water color paper come in imperial size 30" x 22" (762mm x 559mm). One sheet folded and cut into four will provide paper for four medium sized water color paintings. Many years ago paper was handmade and such paper can still be obtained today. However, in recent years machinery has enabled the manufature of mould-made water color paper. Winsor and Newton produce two excellent water color papers, a cotton rag Artists Water Color Paper and their Cotman Water Color Paper.

Both are of fine quality, with the Cotman paper being the less expensive. These popular papers can be obtained in sheet, sketch book, or block form. You can cut the sheets to whatever size that you require. The water color sketch books are usually spiral bound. The water color blocks come as a number of sheets mounted on a stiff backing board and gummed at the sides of the block. The paper on the blocks, if the painting is carried out on the block, does not require stretching. The sheet is carefully removed at the end of the painting. The technique of stretching is described in the next section. Water color painting boards are also available. The board has a sheet of water color paper glued to the surface and can be cut to any size you require.

Watercolor Paper

Stretching paper

Water color washes can cause paper to wave and distort when applied to the paper. Artists overcome this by stretching or pre-shrinking their water color paper to eliminate the likelihood of the paper wavering. For this you will require a wooden drawing board, or piece of ply board, measuring not less than 18"x14" (457mm x 356mm). The board needs to have a matt wooden finish, not varnished or painted white, as the gummed tape will not stick to these surfaces. Cut a sheet of water color paper at least 2" (50mm) smaller than the board. Run the paper under the cold water tap soaking both sides thoroughly. Let the surplus water drain off the paper surface, then lay the wet paper on your board. Use a clean, dry tissue to wipe a 1/2" (13mm) edge of the paper along all four sides. The edge should look matt, the wetness of the rest of the paper should glisten. Cut strips of your 1(25mm) wide gummed paper and wet them. Stick half the width of each strip onto the edges of the paper and half the width firmly on to the board. Let the gummed paper dry for five minutes. The paper will start to waver and distort. You can either leave the board with the paper on to dry at room temperature or, after five minutes, use a hair dryer to gently dry the paper. Leave the dry paper taped on the board and paint your picture on it, removing the picture at the end. Now the painting will be on a flat unwavering sheet of paper. I certainly recommend you stretch the first sheets of 90lb. (190gsm) and 140lb. (300gsm) paper as you prepare to work on them. Then, if you are not covering more than 50% of the paper with a painting, or not working wet, you can work on these papers without stretching them. The heavier weights of paper, from 260lb. (555gsm) upward, rarely need stretching.

Wet water color paper

Wipe edges

Tape down

Dry with hairdryer or at room temperature

Miscellaneous Materials

Your Watercolor Kit:

Your kit comes with the following basic
components

Brushes:
1 x ½" flat wash brush
1 x No. 10 round
1 x No. 6 round
1 x No. 4 round

Paints- Tubes:
Alizarin Crimson
Ultramarine Blue
Cadmium Yellow
Payne's Gray
Burnt Sienna
Cadmium Red
Hooker's Green
Burnt Umber
Yellow Ochre
Cerulean Blue
Permanent white gouache
Pack of twelve watercolor pencils

Pencils:
HB and 2B

Sharpener
Sandpaper
Felt tipped pen

Paper:
sheets of watercolor paper — natural white

Other:
white plastic "slant well" palette

Optional items:
These do not come in your kit but are
readily available around the house or in an
art supply store:
- small genuine sponge
- 2 containers for water
- a solid drawing board (ie: wood) about
18" x 14" (460mm x 350mm)
- scratch pad or scrap paper pad
- soft tissues for blotting
- bottle of black India ink and dip-in pen
- masking fluid
- toothbrush
- tinted watercolor paper
- 2B pencil
- kneaded putty eraser
- gummed paper tape

Washes

It is a good idea to spend a few moments experimenting with your paints, paper and brushes to learn the different types of washes and how to apply them. This will help ensure your paintings looking fresh, clear and have the lovely translucent effect which is such a feature of water color painting.

A flat wash.

This is just a mixture of water and color applied evenly. Use a round brush and mix water and a little ultramarine blue together on your palette. Apply brush strokes of the same length, letting each brush stroke touch the previous one. Do not rub or scrub with your paint brush. Do not go back over the brush strokes.

A graduated wash.

Using your 1/2" (13mm) flat wash brush make a stronger mixture of Ultramarine blue and water on your palette. Apply your first stroke from left to right and then add a little more water to the mixture and apply the second stroke to just touch the first stroke. Keep repeating this, reducing the mixture a little each time. Lightening a wash from dark to light, or adding color and darkening, has many uses in water color painting.

Hard edge and wet on wet washes.

Paint three strokes of burnt umber on the dry surface of your paper. The brush strokes stay just as you painted them. These are known as hard edge washes. Sometimes softer atmospheric effects are needed.

Wet the surface of your paper with a little clean water. Apply three similar brush strokes. The color will diffuse and spread. This is known as "wet wash" — wet paint on the surface of the wet paper or a wet painting. If you apply a water color wash onto a piece of newspaper, no matter how dark the wash, it should be translucent enough to see newsprint through it.

Brush strokes.

Experiment with your round and flat brushes. Use them full of color and water, see how many different strokes you can create. Try them with very little water so that your brush seems to be running out of water. Brush strokes made with the brush like this are known as dry brush technique and have many uses. Try stippling, painting dots of color. Try gently jabbing your paint brush at the surface of the paper. You will be surprised just how many effects you can create.

Experiment... and have fun.

Color

Color Mixing

The practical and indispensable color charts on these pages help guide learning to mix colors.

The first chart shows how the three *Primary Colors*. Red, yellow and blue, make the three *Secondary Colors*, orange, mauve and green. The secondary colors can be mixed to make the three *Tertiary Colors*, dark brown, light brown and olive green.

How to Make Black

Three primary colors mixed together produce black. I generally advise people not to use black paint to darken a color. It seems to dull and deaden the colors and they lose their clarity.

Complementary Color Wheel

Black is opposite, or complementary, to white. Each color has its opposite color, shown on the *Complemetary Color Wheel* — black/white; yellow/mauve; orange/blue; red/green.

It is a good idea to ask yourself what is the predominant color of your subject and to try to have a splash of the opposite color in the painting. This can have a dramatic effect. If you mix any two opposite or complementary colors together in equal amounts, you produce grey.

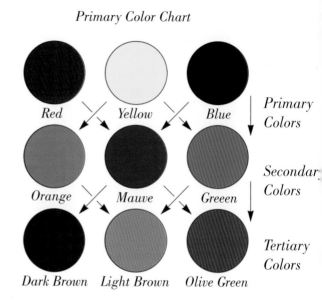

Primary Color Chart

Red   Yellow   Blue   Primary Colors

Orange   Mauve   Green   Secondary Colors

Dark Brown   Light Brown   Olive Green   Tertiary Colors

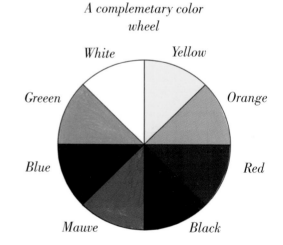

A complemetary color wheel

White   Yellow   Greeen   Orange   Blue   Red   Mauve   Black

Color

The Color Tint Chart

Group your colors in the way I show. Paint a strong tone of the color in the first of the three boxes then make a medium tone made by adding a little white paint, then a light tone by adding even more white. This will show you the color and two of its lighter shades.

Greens Color Chart

This shows how with three blues, three yellows, one green, and white, you can make twenty-five greens of value to anyone who paints, but especially to the landscape and floral painter. If you paint the charts on paper cut to A4 size, when dry, they can be placed in a clear plastic folder to keep them clean, ready for you to refer to when painting.

Color Tint Chart

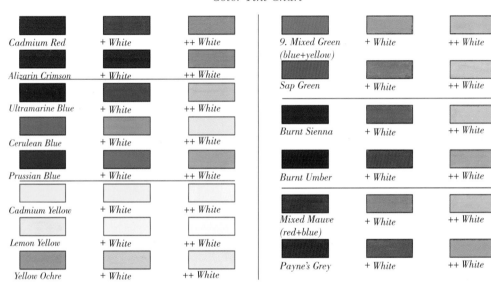

Cadmium Red	+ White	++ White
Alizarin Crimson	+ White	++ White
Ultramarine Blue	+ White	++ White
Cerulean Blue	+ White	++ White
Prussian Blue	+ White	++ White
Cadmium Yellow	+ White	++ White
Lemon Yellow	+ White	++ White
Yellow Ochre	+ White	++ White

9. Mixed Green (blue+yellow)	+ White	++ White
Sap Green	+ White	++ White
Burnt Sienna	+ White	++ White
Burnt Umber	+ White	++ White
Mixed Mauve (red+blue)	+ White	++ White
Payne's Grey	+ White	++ White

Green Color Chart

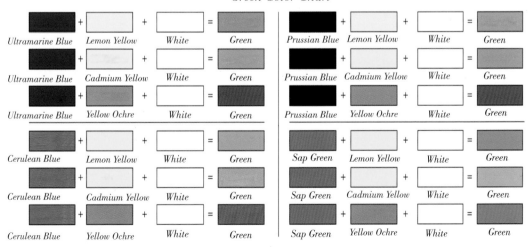

Ultramarine Blue	+ Lemon Yellow	+ White	= Green
Ultramarine Blue	+ Cadmium Yellow	+ White	= Green
Ultramarine Blue	+ Yellow Ochre	+ White	= Green
Cerulean Blue	+ Lemon Yellow	+ White	= Green
Cerulean Blue	+ Cadmium Yellow	+ White	= Green
Cerulean Blue	+ Yellow Ochre	+ White	= Green

Prussian Blue	+ Lemon Yellow	+ White	= Green
Prussian Blue	+ Cadmium Yellow	+ White	= Green
Prussian Blue	+ Yellow Ochre	+ White	= Green
Sap Green	+ Lemon Yellow	+ White	= Green
Sap Green	+ Cadmium Yellow	+ White	= Green
Sap Green	+ Yellow Ochre	+ White	= Green

Landscape

Throughout this book I will demonstrate a variety of subjects for you to try. A water color painting is normally built up by applying the lightest tones of each color, letting them dry, overlaying a second, layer of medium tones, and when dry adding the third, darker tones of each color. Finally the detail is added. This traditional technique is the best way to learn control of your water colors and provide a good base on which to develop other techniques.

Stage 1. Stretch a piece of your water color paper measuring not less than 14" by 10" (356mm x 254mm). When the paper is dry use your 2B pencil to sketch out the view as shown in this demonstration. Always decide where the light source is coming from to light your subject. We will imagine the sunlight is coming from the right hand side so the shadows will fall to the left.

Stage 2. Use a pale wash of ultramarine blue and apply the first wash for the sky with your largest round brush. Leave white paper showing for the white clouds. Use pale blue and mauve for the distant hills. Mix a pale green from cadmium yellow and ultramarine blue and apply a pale wash of green for the fields and tree foliage. Let these dry and add a pale wash of Burnt Umber to the path and tree trunk.

Stage 3. When dry, add a medium tone of each color to the areas you see in my stage three picture. Use a little less water and a little more color to make these medium tones. Leave some of the paler tones showing through.

Stage 4. When dry, add a darker tone to each area as in my stage four painting. The picture is beginning to build up. Now comes the part where everything falls into place.

Stage 5. Use a medium, or small, round brush and put in the details: the hedges detail to the tree trunk, boughs and branches, the fence, edges of the grass as it comes to the path, and, using a slightly dry brush with green on it, create a grass texture. Your painting should now be finished. Have a spare piece of paper at the side of your painting, so that as you mix your colors you can test them on the paper, before applying them to your painting.

Stage 1

Stage 2

Stage 3

Landscape

Stage 4

Stage 5

Monochrome Lakeland Bridge

The understanding and application of tone in painting is of great importance. This aspect of painting is not difficult to understand. In Great Britain, during the Victorian period of the mid to late 1800s, art tutors were keen to encourage their students to understand tone by painting monochrome studies. Monochrome means mono (one), chrome (colour): one colour. They often used Sepia, a gentle brown colour. While very few people I encounter today seem to be taught the techniques of monochrome painting I consider it an essential and very enjoyable aspect of learning to paint. It helps the development of fine painting skills. Try this demonstration of the Bridge House at Windermere in the English Lake District.

Stage 1. Lightly sketch out the subject using a 2B pencil.

Stage 2. Mix burnt umber with water to a pale tone and apply the first washes with your large and medium brushes. Let the washes dry.

Stage 3. Mix a medium tone of burnt umber and apply the washes of this tone as shown. Notice that in some areas the paler tone is left to show through. Let the washes dry.

Stage 4. Mix a darker tone of the color and apply the third tonal washes. Again, some of the paler and medium washes are allowed to show through as they become an important part of the painting. At this stage the painting should start to come together.

Stage 5. Use a number 2, or 3, round brush and, with a fourth darker tone, created by using more color and less water, pick out and add detail. This technique is invaluable in the process of learning to paint successful water colors. Look around you over the coming weeks and see how many examples of monochromes you can find. Black and white newspaper photographs, black and white television pictures, the blue willow pattern on china and many patterns and designs for bathroom and kitchen tiles are all examples of monochrome (one colour in different tones) at work around you.

Before you start your monochrome, use a spare piece of paper and mix the four tones of burnt umber and paint them onto the paper. Mix light, medium, dark and very dark. These can then be used to test each wash as you work, before applying the wash to the painting.

Stage 1

Monochrome Lakeland Bridge

Stage 2

Stage 3

Stages 4 and 5, the details make the completed painting.

River Edge at Dawn

Water colors can be applied to wet paper to create most appealing atmospheric background effects. To understand the dramatic effects which can be achieved we stay with monochrome painting but use a color called Payne's grey. This is a strong, bluish grey. As we work with the paper very wet in areas, I suggest you stretch a piece of 140lb paper.

Stage 1. Wet the top two thirds of your stretched paper with clean water. Leave the bottom third dry.

Stages 2 and 3. Mix Payne's grey and water and drip it across the top of the wet paper. Pick your board up and quickly tip it from side to side, then tip it up vertically. Let the colour spread.

Stage 4. Repeat stages 2 and 3 quickly while the sky is still damp. This should ensure the sky is darker at the top and paler as it comes lower down the page.

Stage 5. Following the above stages 1 to 4, your sky should look as shown here.

Stage 6. While the sky is damp use a pale tone of Payne's grey and, with your No. 10 or 12 round brush, add the first stages and reflections of the reeds and the first effect of the river. Let the painting dry.

Stage 7. Now, using medium and darker tones of Payne's grey and a number 3 round brush, use the traditional hard edge technique and add the tree, fence, birds, finished effects of the reeds, riverside bank and effects on the river. With the hard edge technique the brush mark or line stays where you place it. With the wet wash technique the color spreads and softens.

Stage 8. This is how the finished painting should look.

Water colours dry by evaporation. If you are working wet and need an area to dry a little more quickly, you can use a hair dryer to speed up the process.

Stage 1

Stage 2

Stage 3

Stage 4

River Edge at Dawn

Stage 5

Stage 6

River Edge at Dawn

Stage 7

Stage 8

Sky and Cloud Techniques

It is often said the best things in life are free. We are surrounded by so many beautiful gifts of nature that it is easy to take them for granted. Nature's gifts are free for us to enjoy, and, for those of us who paint, to record for the enjoyment of others. When we look at a photograph the sky is static, frozen by the camera, unmoving. Yet stand for a few moments and look at the real sky, with clouds in it, on a gentle, sunlit day or a blustery, cold day. You will see the sky and clouds have a moving, ever changing nature. The skies of the four seasons, spring, summer, autumn and winter are so different. The height of the clouds, the strength of any prevailing wind, the varying strength of sunlight, the dryness or dampness of the day, all affect the sky. Nature offers the painter skies of tranquility and warmth to scenes of great drama. Skies are one of the greatest free shows on earth.

I show a series of demonstration skies which I suggest you try. These will help you explore the painting of skies and open up the possibilities skies offer to the landscape painter. They will help impart a freshness to your painting. Selecting just the right blue from your palette is important in achieving the right atmospheric effect. The blue for a hot summer's day is quite different from the blue required for a blustery autumn day.

I've shown a blues color chart which is well worth making out on a spare sheet of paper. As you look at your chart, look at the sky, plan to paint, or form part of your landscape, and achieve just the right coloring. I show how, if you have three blues, ultramarine, cerulean blue and Prussian blue, and paint three tones of each, you have nine blues and tints to select from. I also show how adding a small amount of alizarin crimson can make a mauvish blue, or a small amount of burnt umber can make a cool, greyish blue. I show how the paler tints of blue, with the addition of a small amount of burnt sienna, can make very gentle greys, ideal for the soft and medium greys found in billowy cumulus type clouds.

Make out the chart, and then use it to help paint the following sky demonstrations.

Blues colour tint chart

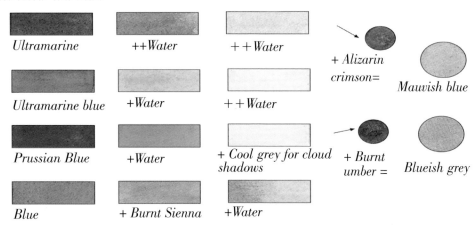

Lifting Out Clouds

This painting is of a gentle landscape, with light, billowy clouds coming up towards us from the horizon in a cool, blue sky.

Stage 1. Using your flat wash brush paint a graduated wash of ultramarine blue.

Stage 2. Crumple up a ball of clean, damp tissue. While the sky is still wet, dab and jab the damp tissue ball on the sky and it will create very convincing clouds.

Stage 3. Sketch in, and with your round brushes, paint the landscape. Note how the stronger tones of blue towards the top of the sky, and the stronger tones of green in the foreground of the fields help to create an illusion of distance, with the colors softening as they recede.

Stage 1

Stage 2

Stage 3

High Fleeting Clouds

This is the type of day when one wants to wear the lightest of shirts or blouses and to enjoy the warm sunlight. The sky has just a hint of fleeting clouds.

Stage 1. Apply a graduated wash of Cerulean Blue with your flat brush.

Stage 2. While the sky is still wet, use the ball of damp tissue technique described in the previous demonstration to lift out a few fleeting clouds in the way I show.

Stage 3. Let the sky dry. Sketch and paint in the landscape with your round brushes. Note how I use three tall poplar trees to help give the added effect of recession to the landscape

Stage 1

Stage 2

Stage 3

A Fused Coloured Sky

Skies often have more than just one color in them. Some skies have clearly defined clouds and cloud masses, others can be hazy, atmospheric skies with no clouds, but with a variety of hints of colors within them. In this demonstration we use the wet wash technique as shown in the "River Edge at Dawn" demonstration, but with two colours in the sky.

Stage 1. Wet the top half of the page with clean water. Mix and brush in a little cerulean blue, leaving some areas of white paper.

Stage 2. As the colour spreads, and while still wet, mix a little alizarin crimson. Touch a few brush marks of this color onto the wet blue sky. The colors will fuse and soften giving a delightful effect. Let the sky dry.

Stage 3. Sketch in and paint the lansdcape. Note how with the foreground lake I have picked up some of the reflected sky colors on the surface of the lake. I have also used a small fence on the left to help take the eyes into the picture from the left hand side.

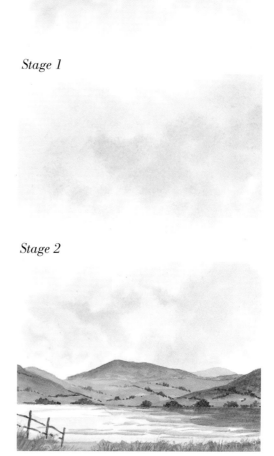

Stage 1

Stage 2

Stage 3

23

A Storm At Sea

Now for a really dramatic sky. In this painting I use a little summer sky in the top right hand corner, but want to achieve the effect of a storm brewing up at sea, with the heavy nimbus-like clouds rising up from the left hand bottom corner and side of the horizon. It is the type of impending storm when any ship's captain would look for the nearest port or harbor.

Stage 1. Paint a pale wash of cerulean blue in the top right hand corner of the sky. Let it dry.

Stage 2. Using a large round brush, or a large flat brush, paint a medium tone wash of Prussian Blue from the left, just up to, and just over, the dry first stage. Let it dry. Then mix Prussian blue with a little burnt umber to make the dark, heavier blue and paint the storm clouds upwards and across the sky from the left and the horizon.

Stage 3. Using pale and medium tones of Prussian blue, paint in the sea, which should look as though it is just becoming choppy, leaving white flecks of paper to add to this effect. With a No. 3 or 6 round brush add the ship to the left of centre and the headland to the right on the horizon.

Stage 1

Stage 2

Stage 3

Niarbyl Bay - Isle of Man

What you leave out of a painting is as important as what you put in. I have had the enjoyment of painting and demonstrating in some of the most glorious and paintable locations on earth. One of my favourite locations is on the Isle of Man, on the west coast of England, just south of the town of Peel. It is Niarbyl Bay. A group of white cottages nestles beneath the cliffs just a few yards from the sea.

Although I painted this view from life, sitting at the bay, I did take some photographs so that you could see the original location and could see what I put in and what I left out. I left out the modern addition of the black and white building to the right of the cottages, the washing by the left of the door and the cars. I selected the angle of the cottages, but found by walking back some 20 metres .

I could use the small, curving sea wall and foreground grass on the right to add to the composition. The wall takes the eyes in, towards the cottages. The upturned boat was in the position you see and the seagull just happened to sit on the wall while I was painting. The figures were holiday makers who came to see what I was painting. I asked the father and son if they would go and stand in the spot you now see them and look out to sea so that I could paint them into the picture to add human interest.

A camera is a handy tool, artists can do more than the camera. The camera could not leave the washing out but I did. This painting encompasses all I have so far taught you. If you try this demonstration, you should be well on the way to a real understanding of painting with water colors.

Photographs of subject

Niarbyl Bay - Isle of Man

Stage 1. Sketch out the subject lightly with a 2B pencil.

Stage 2. Using a large round or flat wash brush, paint in the first light washes for each area or item. The sky is a mixture of ultramarine and cerulean blue. For the grass use hooker's green. For the cliffs use a mixture of pale yellow ochre and burnt sienna. For the sea use pale ultramarine. The grey of the wall, roadway and grey cliff area are a mix of ultramarine and burnt umber.

Stage 3. Build up the medium tones of each area and each item.

Stage 4. With your No. 3 or No. 6 round brush add the darker tones. Add the details to the thatch, rocks, sea, wall, grass, boat and figures.

While I encourage people to work from life whenever possible, often people wish to learn to paint indoors first, particularly if the weather is inclement. The demonstrations in this book will be of real help to you if you try them out. Now start to look through magazines, calendars and your own family photographs to see if you can find several subjects you could paint. This will allow you to try out the techniques you will have learned from my demonstrations. It will also enable your own individual style to start to show in your paintings.

Stage 1

Niarbyl Bay - Isle of Man

Stage 2

Stage 3

Niarbyl Bay - Isle of Man

Stage 4

Tree Techniques

There are several mini demonstrations I like people to try key to learning to paint almost any type of tree.

You should always remember that trees are living, growing things. Most trees change with the season. Trees should always look as though birds could fly in and out of them. One should always be conscious of the general shape of the tree, its age, and the season that you are painting it in, spring, summer, autumn or winter. In the first tree demonstration panel below I show trees in their winter state, with no foliage.

Note with the younger of the two tree trunks how I use a round brush and paint the brush strokes upward from the ground and outward from the trunk. Trees grow upwards, not downwards. As the tree grows, each part of the trunk, boughs, and branches become thicker lower down and get thinner the higher or further away you get from the trunk and boughs. Always remember thicker getting thinner. Tree trunks, especially older tree trunks, can make marvellous subjects with great character. Try these two water color sketches and then see if you can find examples of your own to paint.

Tree trunks start thicker at the bottom and become thinner as they grow upwards. The same applies to boughs and branches.

Winter trees

Tree trunk textures vary widely and make good subjects to paint.

A fan brush can be used in a dry brush technique to create winter or summer trees, depending on the colour of paint used.

29

Tree Techniques

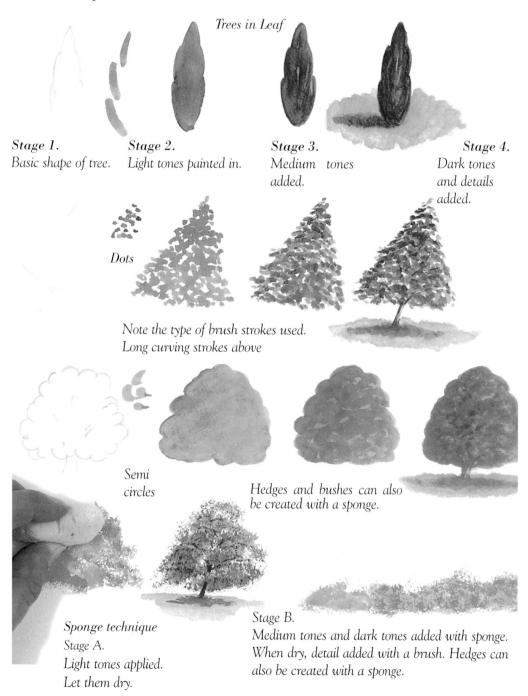

Trees in Leaf

Stage 1.
Basic shape of tree.

Stage 2.
Light tones painted in.

Stage 3.
Medium   tones
added.

Stage 4.
Dark tones
and details
added.

Dots

Note the type of brush strokes used.
Long curving strokes above

Semi
circles

Hedges and bushes can also
be created with a sponge.

Sponge technique
Stage A.
Light tones applied.
Let them dry.

Stage B.
Medium tones and dark tones added with sponge.
When dry, detail added with a brush. Hedges can
also be created with a sponge.

Around the Home

So far we have looked at landscape subjects. If you have tried the demonstrations you should already have learned some very useful techniques which can also be applied to a wide range of other subjects. You should also be gaining confidence in your own painting skills. Now look around you, around your home, in fact in the very room you are reading this book. You will find subjects all around you. Often the every day items we take for granted can make ideal subjects to sketch and paint. In my lounge is a trophy my daughter won for public speaking. In a kitchen cupboard I found an everyday coffee jug. Both proved interesting to paint. See if you can find one or two individual subjects you can try to paint from life. What I do strongly recommend is that you start to keep

a water colour sketch book. A medium sized spiral bound sketch pad, with 140lb 'NOT' water color paper is ideal as you can flip the finished sheets over to reveal the next page, yet all the pages remain intact in the spiral bound sketch pad. Just wander around your home looking for subjects and add a new subject to the sketch pad every day or so. Fruit, vegetables, ornaments, books, potted plants and fresh flowers, workbox tools, everyday objects provide a wealth of material for you to paint. Van Gogh painted a chair and a pair of boots. If he found this worthwhile it should commend itself to us also. Look for small objects like -a key or watch and paint them up larger than life size. Try reducing some larger items to a smaller size. Experiment. This is a good way of introducing you to painting from life.

Trawler

There are a range of water color techniques including a little known one of combining water colours and pencil. While the pencil is often used for sketching the subject out prior to painting, the pencil can be used on top of the finished water color to achieve a subtly different effect. In the demonstration of the trawler which I found in Peel Harbour on the Isle of Man, I show the traditional pencil sketch. On the right hand side of the sketch I have added the main water colour washes. I did not add the finishing details with my paint brush, but used a 2B soft pencil to oversketch the painting, adding and emphasising the textures of the rocks, grass and detail of the trawler.

In the technique used for the trawler the whole subject is painted in water colors, but another variation of the technique, which can make for highly distinctive studies is shown in the pencil and water color study of the tulip opposite. In this technique, the stem and leaves of the flower are sketched and shaded to a finished stage using a 2B pencil. The tulip head is painted in water color and oversketched in pencil. There is no reason why you should not mix the media in this way if it will give you the effect you seek. I have painted studies of birds in which the branch and foliage the bird is sitting on are in pencil, and the bird, the main subject of the picture, has been painted in water colors. Always be prepared to experiment.

Stage 1

Stage 2

Stage 3

Tulip — Pencil and Watercolor

Try out both of the variations of the pencil and water color technique, adding them to your increasing repertoire of techniques you are now buiding up.

Stage 1.
I picked this tulip from our garden. The stem and leaves are sketched out and finished using a 2B pencil. The tulip head is only lightly sketched out.

Stage 2.
The tulip head is painted with water colors and when dry oversketched in pencil.

Pen and Wash

Pen and wash is one of the most enjoyable avenues of water color painting. It allows you to produce quick color sketches of subjects or finished art work. When nine years old I recall the class teacher telling the whole art class not to put black lines around everything. Children often do this to make things stand out, instead of using perspective and light and shade to achieve the same effect. Pen and wash pictures are where the artist uses a black pen and ink, or a fine nylon or felt-tip pen, to oversketch the subject to achieve a distinctive effect. Pen and ink usually refers to the use of a dip-in type pen with a metal nib together with a bottle of black waterproof Indian ink. It is possible to buy mapping pens and drawing pens singularly or in a set. These are obtainable from most art shops or stationers. I like the dip-in type nib. It allows you to vary the thickness of the line by altering the amount of pressure you apply to the pen. It allows for a considerable degree of expression of line on the artists part. It is possible to buy waterproof nylon or fine felt-tip pens which are wonderful to use in situations where it may not be convenient to use a dip-in pen and ink. Generally speaking, the ink in these pens is not light fast and can be subject to fading over a period of time if exposed to strong day light. Indian Ink is permanent, waterproof and light fast. There are a number of technical drawing pens on the market. These are used by architects and draughtsmen and many artists also enjoy using them. The line produced is the thickness of the nib used. Different thicknesses of nib are available and these are interchangeable.

You can be inventive and use a cocktail stick or even sharpen a piece of bamboo cane. These all offer distinctive, individual types of mark or line.

This small sketch of Tuscany was produced in just five minutes. Quick outdoor sketches in this technique can provide original coloured sketches, enabling the artist to paint larger, finished pictures from them in the studio if there has been insufficient time to paint the finished picture on location.

Water mill

I discovered this delightful water-mill one summer's afternoon on a walk through a glen in the Isle of Man. Do not have too much ink on your dip-in pen nib. Too much ink can lead to blots. Test the pen nib each time you dip into the ink on a piece of scrap paper.

Stage 1. Sketch the subject out with a 2B pencil on 1401b. "NOT" water color paper.

Stage 2. Paint in the light, medium and dark tones for each area using the methods described in the earlier chapters of this book. Do not paint in the details. Leave the water color at the three quarters finished stage.

Stage 3. Use a dip-in pen, or a nylon or felt-tip pen, to oversketch the subject. The result should be fresh, crisp and eye-catching.

Stage 2

Stage 1

Stage 3

Villa Pitiana

Many people have the opportunity each year to go on holiday. While the country we live in provides a wealth of subjects, the advent of modern forms of travel, especially air travel, offer us the opportunity to visit foreign countries, which in many instances our parents and grandparents could only read about or see photographs of.

On one occasion, I had the good fortune to hold one of my painting holiday courses at the Villa Pitiana in Tuscany, to the east of Florence. This 12th-century former palace, bathed in warm sunlight, offered the perfect subject for a pen and wash study. I used a sheet of 140lb HP, smooth water colour paper. The colours used were cerulean blue, hooker's green, yellow ochre, lemon yellow, ultramarine, burnt umber and scarlet lake. Water color paper comes in three textures. "HP" Hot pressed, or smooth, is ideal for detailed work and pen and wash studies. "ROUGH" is not suited to pen and wash work. "NOT" water color paper is neither rough nor smooth, but also lends itself to pen and wash work.

Stage 1. Sketch the subject out using a 2B pencil.

Stage 2. Paint in the sky using a wet wash technique with cerulean blue. Use the same pale blue on the olive trees.

Use a mix of pale hooker's green for the pale green area of foliage and fields. Paint a mix of the same green with a little cerulean blue added for the darker tones of the foliage behind the palace. Use lemon yellow with hooker's green for the right hand light tree. Use hooker's green with ultramarine and burnt umber for the darker trees. Mix a little yellow ochre and lemon yellow for the painted wall plaster of the palace. Use scarlet lake and lemon yellow for the roof. A pale mix of ultramarine and burnt umber will provide the pale grey of the stone walls and palace stone work. Paint a bluish grey from ultramarine and burnt umber for the road.

Stage 3. Oversketch with pen and ink.

Stage 1

Villa Pitiana

Stage 2

Stage 3

Portrait on a Train

I was sitting on a train one day returning from Manchester to Southport, when at Wigan station this wonderful character, a workman who had just finished his shift, came and sat down on the seat across the aisle. I had my sketching materials handy and produced this felt-tip pen and wash sketch. His rugged face, work-worn hands and the dark browns and black of his clothes made him an exciting subject to paint. The speed of the felt-tip pen and wash method enabled me to sketch this in ten minutes, just before he reached his station and left the train.

A Doll

Most fathers of young daughters like to buy them dolls, and if they travel abroad they often bring back dolls in the national costume of the country they have been to. My daughter Penelope now has quite a collection. I came across this little fellow on a visit to Dallas and Houston. His impish smile and colorful clothes immediately caught my eye. He also shows that even children's toys can provide exciting material to paint. I sketched him out in pencil, added the colors, then used my fine felt-tip pen to oversketch him.

Perspective

Perspective is the one area of drawing and painting in which most people experience some degree of difficulty. When most people hear perspective mentioned they go to a bookshop or a library, obtain a book on the subject, flip through it, see lines shooting about all over, and usually end up more confused than before.

The secret is to keep the whole business of perspective as simple as possible, to remember a few basic rules, and to bear in mind that perspective is not something one masters all in one, two, or three lessons. Learning about perspective is an on-going learning process. One goes along over a period of months, indeed years, collecting together the pieces of information, like pieces of a jigsaw, until they all fit together and the picture, the theory of perspective, becomes clear and easy to apply to one's work.

The eyelevel is an imaginary line, horizontally across your field of vision when you look straight ahead, not up, nor down, but straight ahead.

In my sketch, I show a figure sitting low down, as if on a beach, then standing, then standing on a sand dune (*fig. 1*). Note how the eyelevel is always directly ahead of the figure.

When looking at a real subject look straight ahead, hold a ruler straight out with the thin edge in front of, and across your eyes, and that is where your eyelevel is. Which comes first, the drawing in of the eyelevel or the object? Generally I suggest you draw in the object lightly first, then apply the eyelevel and use it with the rules of perspective to check and correct the object. One way to see perspective in action is to picture the view looking along railway lines. They appear to merge in the distance. They appear to become smaller and closer together. The point where they appear to merge is known as the *vanishing point*. We know they do not merge in reality. I show this in my sketch (*fig. 2*). I also show the railway lines with telegraph poles on the left, then with three trees on the right. The telegraph poles and the trees in a drawing or painting would also appear to become smaller and closer together as they recede.

I have shown the guidelines for each item, illustrating how the guidelines meet at the vanishing point.

Perspective

fig. 1

Eyelevel

fig. 2

Vanishing Point

VP

Perspective

Next I show a front view of a chair. With this view there is just one vanishing point on the horizon line for the sides of the box. I am imagining that I am sitting on another chair at a table, drawing the chair in front of me. If I look straight ahead, over the box, my horizon line would be about 12" (30.5cm) above the top of the tool box. In my next sketch the box is set at an angle. We now have two vanishing points, one for each side. Guidelines will often converge at vanishing points off the page. This is quite normal and often happens. When it does, lay scrap paper at the side and tape it on from behind, then extend the guidelines onto it, in the way I show in my sketch. Never guess or assume the perspective is correct, always try to prove it.

Vanishing Point

fig. 3

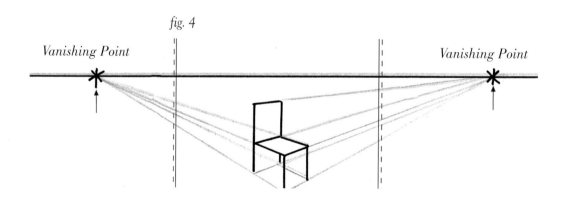

fig. 4

Vanishing Point   *Vanishing Point*

Circular Perspective

Few people realize that perspective helps to solve the problems of drawing circles and ellipses, but it can. I have illustrated this in a sketch of a bottle and glasses with one on its side (fig. 5). I have lightly drawn the group out and have placed my eyelevel well above it. I have then drawn a light guiding square around each ellipse we can see and have drawn those squares 'in perspective', in the same way as the television. The squares for the ellipses each have their respective vanishing points on the common eyelevel. The glasses share the same vanishing point as their ellipses are on the same plane.

The use of the squares helps determine where each vanishing point should be, to ensure the true perspective of the subject where there is an ellipse involved. I then go back to each ellipse and check if it touches the centre of each side of the square it occupies, for provided it does, I know the ellipse must be in perspective. Gently rub out the squares used outside of each ellipse and perspective guidelines before a picture is shaded in or painted.

fig. 5

Vanishing Point

Vanishing Point

Composition

There are certain guidelines that help build work on sound compositional foundations. One of the most important things to avoid is having any line or object that cuts your picture into two equal halves. Set any such line or object to one side or other.

Focal points and key lines

Decide what it is that you want the viewer to look at. Ensure their eyes will not wander, as if the viewer is lost. You are the artist, you are in control, be decisive.

A picture should have a focal point, that is, a main feature to which the eye may draw. I show three views. In the first, the focal point, the cottage, is in the middle distance. In the second, the focal point, the ship, is in the far distance. In the third the fisherman in the foreground is the focal point.

A picture should also have key lines of the composition leading the eyes of the viewer to the focal point. I have arrowed the key lines of the three compositions and I think from these illustrations you will see how the use of the focal point and key lines help bring a composition together.

Halfway

Halfway

Halfway

Halfway

45

Composition

The Triangle

Often a triangle can offer an excellent shape on which to base a composition, especially a still life or floral study. I have shown a still life made up from a group of toys. I have placed the teddy bear to the right so the apex of the triangle is off-centre. The rose in the vase forms the upright of the triangle, with the handbag and powder compact forming the base. The tree creates the triangle's upright side, with the landscape and church forming the bottom and third, sloping side, of the triangle. Try to ensure that still life and floral studies have height, width, and depth to them. If you now go and look at paintings, or prints of paintings, by any of the great masters, or by any fine artist, you will find that their most successful paintings employ many of the important compositional points that I have referred to here.

Masking Fluid

Masking is a water-based rubber solution used to protect an area of paper, allowing you to paint in a later stage. To show the effects you can achieve using masking fluid, I've shown a duck on a lake. If I simply drew the duck and painted the lake water up to it, the duck would look painted up to, and not have the effect of the water being in front, around, and behind.

Stage 1. Sketch out the duck.

Stage 2. Use masking fluid to cover the shape of the duck. Let the masking fluid dry.

Stage 3. Paint the lake effect over the duck, ignoring it. When the washes are dry, gently rub the masking fluid with a clean fingertip and the masking fluid will peel away, leaving the white duck to be painted in.

Do not let the masking fluid dry on your brush, keep washing it off whilst still wet. Do not use a hair dryer to dry the water color if using masking fluid. Practise using masking fluid on some spare water color paper before using it in a painting.

Stage 1

Stage 2

Stage 3

Gouache

There are water based colors known as gouache, designers colors or poster colors. These are opaque water based colors. During the past century, some artists, such as the great English painter Turner, described them as "Body Color". If painted on newspaper, or colored paper, the paint obliterates the newsprint or colored paper due to the paints opaqueness. Water colors are translucent. This is one of the medium's most distinctive features. To experiment with gouache you do not have to buy a set of gouache paints, because by adding permanent white gouache to your water colors you can make them opaque. Only add enough water to make the paint mixture flow freely off the brush. Do not dilute it as much as for normal water color painting.

An excellent way to arrive at the right degree of opacity for gouache is to try painting the cup below on a piece of newspaper, using permanent white and Prussian blue water colour mixed together. Add a little burnt umber to the blue for the darker tones. Use the technique described over the page.

To discover the difference between water colors and gouache, paint the tree shown using the normal water color technique on water color paper with no white paint. Then try the tree in the gouache technique on a piece of tinted paper. Water colors should be translucent, gouache should be opaque.

Above: Tree. Watercolor

Below: Tree. Gouache

Gouache — Wine Bottle

Here is a simple demonstration of a wine bottle for you to try. I use a piece of maroon paper to achieve my effect; I think it is well worth buying some the next time you are in an art supply store.

Stage 1.
Draw out the subject. Mix the pale green from hookers green water colour and permanent white gouache. Paint the label white.

Stage 2.
Mix medium and darker tones of green for the bottle by adding a little ultramarine and burnt umber to the hookers green on your palette. For the label add a pale grey shadow. Add the table cloth using permanent white gouache and Prussian blue.

Stage 3.
Mix the light yellowy greens and highlights by adding a little lemon yellow and white to the hooker's green and paint these on. Add the shadow for the bottle and the lines on the table cloth. Finally add the hint of detail to the bottle label.

Watercolor Paper — Sunset

Water color paper has traditionally been white to allow the light to be reflected back through the washes applied on it. However I have often been intrigued by the possibility of, and have experimented with, tinting my water color paper all over with a color, then painting my water colour on that tinted paper surface. I show two demonstrations that not only open up this possibility for you, but that helped persuade a major English water color paper manufacturer to produce and extensively market tinted water colour papers.

The first demonstration is a lakeland sunset.

Stage 1. Mix a wash of pale yellow ochre. Apply it with your flat wash brush. Let it dry thoroughly.

Stage 2. Mix a graduated wash of alizarin crimson. Apply the wash from dark to light from the top, and light to dark from the middle to the bottom. Let it dry.

Stage 3. Paint in the middle distance hills and the same shapes reflected in the lake. As you come to the darker tones add a little Payne's grey to the alizarin crimson.

Stage 1

Stage 2

Watercolor Paper — Sunset

Stage 4. Paint in the boats moored at anchor and the foreground grasses on the nearside of the lake.

Stage 3

Stage 4

Watercolor Paper — River View

Part of the fun of painting is to experiment. The medium is as flexible as your imagination. If it surprised you to find me suggesting you used crimson over yellow ochre, let me surprise you even further by suggesting you try hooker's green over yellow ochre.

Stage 1. Paint a wash of pale yellow ochre and let it dry.

Stage 2. Mix a wash of hooker's green and paint an upward curving graduated wash, darker at the top, paler in the middle. Then paint a paler, downward graduated wash, becoming darker at the bottom. Let it dry.

Stage 1

Stage 2

Watercolor Paper — River View

Stage 3. Use a darker tone of the green, paint in the first stages of the trees, island and the river banks.

Stage 4. Mix a little Payne's grey with the hooker's green to make a darker tone, add the details to the trees and boat mooring post. Use the dry brush technique to finish the effects of the grasses in the areas one show.

When you have learned and mastered the basic foundations of water color painting, develop an adventurous nature, be prepared to throw caution to the wind and experiment with the medium; you could be surprised at the results.

Figures

Many people enjoy landscape painting but shy away from adding figures for fear of spoiling the paintings. Figures add human interest and can play an important role in good picture making. It is well worth practising figures on some spare paper to develop a practical approach to painting them.

Moving figures need to look fluid, not rigid. Again, success comes from keeping them simple. In the following demonstration I show a man in a rain coat blown along by the wind and rain, with his umbrella blown inside out. The approach is exactly as in the four stages described above. Do not put in too much detail.

Stage 1   *Stage 2*

Stage 3   *Stage 4*

Figures come in three main groups, foreground figures, middle distance figures and far distant figures. The middle distant figures are the ones you may find most useful. Below I show how to paint static and moving figures. There are many locations where you can practise sketching and painting real, live people. Bus and train stations, markets, cafes and seaside beaches offer a whole host of subjects. If you are unable to go out of doors, thumb through magazines and find examples of the type and size of people I have demonstrated, and practise painting them.

Stage 1. Keep them simple. Sketch the male and female figures out in pencil. Draw a simple head, chest, pelvis and guide lines for the arms and legs.

Stage 2. Make the arms and legs more defined and add the clothes.

Stage 3. Use a medium sized brush and paint a medium wash of color for each part of the figure.

Stage 4. Use a smaller brush and paint a darker tone of each color for the areas of the figures in shadow.

Stage 1   *Stage 2*   *Stage 3*   *Stage 4*

Still Life

Just as styles of handrwriting vary from one person to another, so do styles of painting. A painting by Constable has a very definite and unmistakable look. Leonardo da Vinci's style was totally different to Raphael's, but they were all great masters of painting. In this still life demonstration I show a looser technique for painting with water colors. Instead of sitting down to paint this at a table I stood up. Standing encourages a looser approach and dramatically reduces the temptation to include fiddly detail.

Stage 1. The group was set up and drawn out using a triangular composition. The light comes from a window on the right of the picture.

Stage 2. I set a time limit of 15 minutes so worked quickly. I painted in the light and medium tones with my 1/2" (13mm) flat wash brush and my No. 10 round brush.

Stage 3. I added the darker tones with the point of my No. 10 round brush.

Stage 2

Stage 1

Stage 3

55

Stage 4. Finished still life. Using my No. 6 round brush I added the key dark details to the wine bottle, glass, pineapple and lines of the check tablecloth.

Try this demonstration standing up. Then set up a group of objects of your own choosing and paint that standing up.

Silhouettes — Palm Tree

Back lighting, where the lighting comes from behind the subjects, can be dramatic, as in a sunset. Back lighting can also offer silhouette opportunities. The objects in such pictures appear to lose their natural colour and become very dark. While silhouettes often look black, my advice for silhouettes in a painting is to mix a very dark colour from alizarin crimson, ultramarine and Payne's grey so that the resulting silhouettes are very dark, but have a hint of subtle tonal variations in them, not looking like flat, cut out, paper shapes produced when using black paint. Paint a piece of water colour paper with lemon yellow. Let it dry. Overpaint it with orange and then use alizarin crimson, ultramarine and Payne's grey mixtures to create the tropical sunset with silhouetted palm trees.

Stage 1

Stage 2

Stage 3

Stage 4

Painting with a Toothbrush

Even the humble toothbrush can play a part in painting. Let us stay with the idea of a sunset and use a different technique in a different demonstration.

Stage 1. Place a medium size coin in position to mask out the shape of the sun. Mix lemon yellow and press your toothbrush in the yellow paint. Hold the brush 3" (75mm) above the coin and flick the paint off the toothbrush with your finger by quickly pulling your finger towards you across the toothbrush. Let the paint dry.

Stage 2. Repeat stage one using alizarin crimson, but create a circle of splattered red paint about 2" (50mm) out from the coin by moving your toothbrush away from the coin and flicking round in a circle.

Stage 3. Use India ink and a fine brush to paint in the landscape subject.

Not only is it fun to do, but this is a technique I often use to make greeting cards as the technique can be adapted to a wide range of subjects.

Stage 1

Stage 2

Stage 3

The Camera

Some people frown on the use of a camera and painting from photographs. I believe a camera is a useful tool and can be helpful to the artist. Often when out, due to the shortage of time or the transitory nature of the subject, there may not be time to paint a picture. Take a photograph and use that as the basis for a painting. Another occasion you may see a subject and have time to make a quick sketch. If you also take a photograph you can work from the photograph and sketch in your studio, or at home, to produce your own original painting. I show a sketch below which I did in a boat yard. I took a photograph of the subject for added reference. This combination provided everything to produce a finished painting in my studio.

The colors in a photograph are not 100% accurate. They are a guide for you when painting. Sometimes a part, or a section, of the photograph will make a good subject in its own right. You are in charge, you can select, adapt and use a photograph to create the picture you want. Do not become a slave to photographs but they are a useful aid in the art of painting.

Picture Shapes

Most artists paint their picture up to the edge of their rectangular paper or painting surface. When you see such paintings in an exhibition they often look like postage stamps in an album. Experiment with picture shapes, don't let them become boring. Lay a tea or dinner plate face down on a piece of paper, draw around it, remove the plate and you have a circular format for a painting. Draw a round the top half of a plate to make a semicircle. Add straight sides and a straight baseline and you have another exciting shape to paint in. Buy an oval mount from an art shop.

Lay it on the paper to see the possibilities of a horizontal or vertical painting shape. Try tall, thin paintings and long, thin paintings.

Using a variety of shapes will not only add to your enjoyment of painting, but will often enhance the chance of work being accepted for exhibitions as it adds variety to the standard rectangular shapes so often submitted.

A variety of possible picture shapes

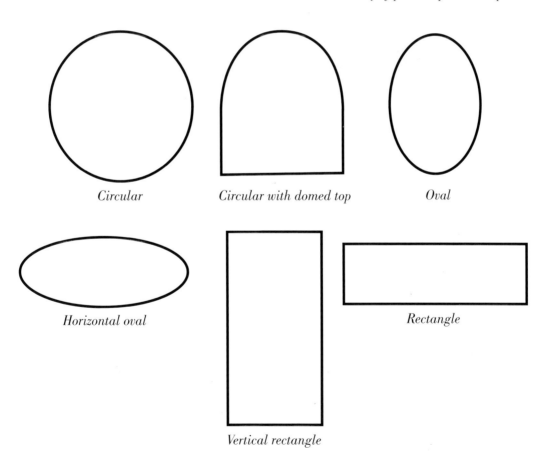

Circular   *Circular with domed top*   *Oval*

Horizontal oval   *Rectangle*

Vertical rectangle

Framing Watercolors

The framing and visual presentation of a water color is very important. Water colors are normally framed, mounted, and placed under glass. The color of the mount chosen not only provides a complementary surround, but also provides an air space between the picture and the protective glass.

Generally I would say that if the painting is light use a darker mounting, if the painting is dark in color and tone use a lighter one.

Try to avoid diffused glass. Although this can take away the reflections of the light on glass it tends to grey the picture and one loses some of the freshness and detail of the work it covers.

While some people like to make their own frames, it is possible to buy very good, inexpensive, ready made frames and mounts from many retail outlets. You can also use the services of a specialist picture framer who will have an extensive range of frames and mount boards. He or she will almost certainly be pleased to help and advise you, and mount and frame your water color for you. This is a personal service like having a suit or dress made for you. The framer's service and expertise will be reflected in the price.

A mount and frame should enhance and complement a painting, not dominate it. You want people to remember the painting, not the frame.